The Lottery Factor:
A Better Way to Win

Bill Karoshi

This book is designed to be used as a guide to assist the reader of the subject matter covered.

© 2019 by Bill Karoshi

Cover Design © 2019 by Bill Karoshi

Published By SIU Press
A division of Sighing In Unison
sighinginunison.com

Executive Editor: Annie O'Sullivan
Executive Consultant: Bryan J Mangam

All rights reserved. No parts of this publication may be reproduced or transmitted in any form or by any means, electronic or mechanical, including photocopying, recording, or any other information storage and retrieval systems, without the written permission of the publisher.

ISBN: 9781095158364

TABLE OF CONTENTS

1 - A Fool's Game — page 7

2 - History of the Lottery — page 19

3 - Morality — page 25

4 - Mentality — page 33

5 - Who Plays the Lottery — page 39

6 - Does the Lottery Bring Pleasure? — page 43

7 - Consequences of Gambling — page 47

8 - The Purpose of the Lottery — page 55

9 - Lottery as Big Business — page 61

10 - The Odds of Winning — page 65

11 - Real Cost to Play the Lottery — page 73

12 - How to Win the Lottery by not Playing — page 81

References — page 89

About the Author — page 91

1

A Fool's Game

"A lottery is properly a tax upon unfortunate self conceited fools. The world abounds in such fools; it is not fit that every man that will may cheat every man that would be cheated. Rather it is ordained that the Sovereign should have guard of these fools, even as in the case of lunatics and idiots."
-Sir William Petty

What is a lottery?

A lottery is a popular form of gambling that involves the drawing of tickets, numbers, and/or names for a fee. The winning ticket/number (or combination of numbers) wins a specified prize. Often times there is more than one prize, thus allowing more than one winner. Generally speaking the lottery is set up in tiers of winners, for example: First, second, third place etc., with the highest winner receiving the largest or best prize. While a few state governments (5) outlaw it, most others endorse it to the extent of organizing a state lottery. The five states that outlaw lotteries are Alabama and Utah for religious reasons, Nevada due to casino competition, Alaska and Hawaii. Among the the legal states it is common to find some degree of regulation of the lottery by state governments (they fall under gambling laws).

The basic definition of gambling is: wagering money on an event with an uncertain outcome and the primary intent of winning additional money.

U.S. Legal Gambling Revenues (2017):

Commercial Casinos	$41.2 Billion
Indian Casinos	$31.95 Billion
Card Rooms	$1.9 Billion
Lotteries	$80.55 Billion
Legal Bookmaking	$248 Million
Pari-Mutuel Wagering	$295 Million
Charitable Games & Bingo	$2.15 Billion
U.S. Grand Total	$158.55 Billion

Source: Center for Gaming Research University Libraries

At the beginning of the twentieth century, most forms of gambling- including lotteries and sweepstakes- were illegal in many countries worldwide, including the United States. This remained in effect until well after World War II. In the 1960's, casinos and lotteries began to appear throughout the world as a means to raise revenue in addition to taxes.

Lotteries are most often described as a regressive tax, since those most likely to buy tickets will typically be the less affluent members of a society. The astronomically high odds against winning have also led to the epithets of a "tax on stupidity," "math tax," or the oxymoron, "voluntary tax" (playing the lottery is voluntary, taxes are not). This is intended to suggest that lotteries, being an addictive form of gambling, are governmental revenue-raising mechanisms that will attract only those consumers who fail to see that playing the game is a very bad deal. The large multi-million dollar prize lotteries in the United States are paid by an annuity over 24-30 years; therefore, if you take the one-time lump sum cash payment, plus pay the federal and local taxes, you will end up with about one third of the total prize money originally promoted.

Lotteries come in many different varieties and formats. The prizes can be a set cash amount or a specific item, such as a car. For set cash or a specific prize, the organizer or administrator of the lottery must ensure that enough tickets are sold to cover the award(s). Lotteries offer the worst odds in legal gambling.

A brief description of some of the lottery games:

The following paragraphs explain the various formats and varieties of the New York Lottery. Other states might have different and similar games of their own. Over the course of time the state lotteries also change the rules of play, or eliminate and add different games.

INSTANT GAMES - Most state lotteries offer a variety of different games. A popular variety of the lottery ticket is the instant game, also known colloquially as *scratch-offs*. To reveal the prizes on these lottery tickets, they contain boxed areas that the participant is required to scratch off. Instant games are faster to find out the results than other lottery types. Typically, in the past, they did not have a large payout value. Today they offer $1 million and higher, including some up to $10- $15 million dollar prizes. Currently, the New York Lottery has over 83 different instant games that are available, ranging from a cost of $1 to $30 per game. Some states (Michigan, and Texas) now even offer $50 instant scratch-offs. Some of these tickets are also payable for life- generally 20 years- but also have a cash value (ex. $2,500 a week for life).

Just a note: some of the individual state lottery websites have a database for their scratch-offs. This database lists what prizes are still available for a particular game. An example is in the New York State $5 instant game called "*$1,000,000 Cashword*" that has four remaining jackpot prizes, while the similarly priced game "*Cash X20*" ($1 million jackpot) has only one remaining jackpot. These numbers change on a daily or weekly basis depending on the state. (As of 11/26/2018).

So if you are going to buy a scratch-off, at least buy one that still has more jackpots and other valuable prizes available to win.

Draw Games:
NUMBERS - "3 Digit Lottery," To play, you pick three numbers and decide on the variation (ex. 123, 321, 231, etc.). If the drawn numbers match your played numbers, then you win. You can play this game in four different wager types: "straight," "box," "straight/box," or "combination." Games are played in either 50 cents or $1 wager amounts and the drawings are played twice daily in the state of New York.

WIN 4 - This game is similar to the Numbers game (Pick 3), except four numbers are selected instead of three. To play, you pick four numbers and use the same wager types as in the Numbers game.

CASH4LIFE - To play, you pick five numbers out of a field of 1-60. You also have to select one out of four "cashball" numbers. Games are twice a week and cost $2 a game. Top prize is $1,000 a day for life, and second prize is $1,000 a week for life. The top prize and second prize will be split or reduced if there are multiple winners. There are also lower prizes for fewer matched number combinations.

TAKE 5 - Five numbers are selected from a field of 1-39. You can win by matching five, four, three, or two numbers. The drawings are announced daily. Costs are $1 per game.

QUICK DRAW - On a Quick Draw play card, you select up to ten numbers ranging from 1-80; you also select your wager from $1 to $10 per game, and how many consecutive games you want to play. Every four minutes a computer randomly selects 20 numbers. How many numbers you match and the amount wagered determines the size of your prize. This game is played daily every four minutes, around the clock, except between 3:25 A.M. and 4:00 A.M. This game is available to play in establishments that sell and serve alcohol.

PICK 10 - Select ten numbers ranging from 1-80. Every night, 20 numbers are randomly selected. If you match 10 out of 20 drawn numbers, you win first prize of $500,000 dollars. There are also prizes for second, third, fourth, and fifth places. The minimum wager to play is $1.

VIDEO LOTTERY TERMINALS (VLTS) or VIDEO LOTTERY GAMES - Video lottery games are basically slot machine type games. Many states allow them at their casinos. They are also available at *Racinos* (horse racing and casino) and Indian Reservation Casinos.

Video Lottery Terminals and Electronic Table Games: Similar in appearance to classic slot machines or as simulated classic table games, these terminals are linked to a centralized system maintained by the Gaming Commission that tracks the game play and earnings for each game.

• Video Lottery Terminals (VLTs) have the same appearance as slot machines. VLTs must receive winning outcomes transmitted by the central system.

• Electronic Table Games (ETGs) offer video versions of popular casino games like roulette, craps, and baccarat. ETGs are capable of generating winning outcomes at each table.

Each machine or terminal in a casino is linked together, forcing players to compete against one another for the prize, and with a set number of wins and losses, the group of machines are programmed to pay out at specific times.

Most video lottery winners are determined much like a lottery scratch-off game. A VLT game starts with a set number of winning and losing "cards" from a "pool." When a player at the gaming machine (terminal) activates a play, the operating system that connects the terminals then randomly selects a "card" from those that remain in the "pool." The operating system then sends the card result, winning or losing ticket (data), back to the respective terminal. The central operating system receives a new "pool" after all the tickets (outcomes) are chosen. There are some variations on VLTs based on locations.

SLOT MACHINES - "Vegas-style" or traditional slots in a casino play independently from other slot machines. The only way in which they are linked is usually in terms of the jackpot, but this is only for progressive networks. Because slot machines use a random number generator (RNG), every machine has exactly the same likelihood of paying out.

For example, a slot machine can have two large jackpots consecutively but a VLT would only give out one jackpot as
another jackpot would not be available until the entire pool is played (used).

Class II casinos generally have VLTs, and Class III Casinos have slot machines.

LARGE JACKPOT LOTTERY GAMES - These games are set up in individual and/ or pooled with multiple states and/or municipalities. They have become very popular because the jackpot prize grows very rapidly and becomes extraordinarily large. They frequently reach $100 million or more, with the current largest jackpot reaching $1.586 billion. For the jackpot, there are two payment options: 25-30 annual payments, or lump sum cash value, which will pay you the current estimated cash value. Please note that this will be less than the advertised value paid for annual payments.

The two main large jackpot lottery games are Mega Millions and Powerball. Their rules vary by jurisdictions.

Many states have their own lottery system and

also offer the multi-state lotteries.

An example of a large jackpot state lottery:
NEW YORK LOTTO - This is the basic lottery variety in New York, which has a large jackpot prize. To play, you pick six numbers ranging from 1-59. The minimum wager is $1 for two game panels. Drawings are bi-weekly on Wednesdays and Saturdays. The payout is available in a lump sum or in an annuity over 25 years (26 payments).

Multi-state run lotteries:
MEGA MILLIONS - This is considered a large jackpot lottery game. Jackpots start at $40 million and increase each game by a minimum of $5 million. To play, you pick five numbers ranging from 1-70 and one *Mega Ball* number ranging from 1-25. Each game costs $2 to play. Currently there are 44 states, plus Washington D.C., and the Virgin Islands participating in the *Mega Millions* lottery. Drawings are bi-weekly on Tuesdays and Fridays at 11:00 EST. The payout is available in a lump sum (cash value) or in an annuity over 30 years.

Cash option: A one-time lump sum payment that is equal to all the cash in the *Mega Millions* jackpot prize pool.
Grand Prize odds are one out of 302,575,350. Some states also offer "Just the Jackpot" option that can be played for $3 for two games. Most participating states offer a *Megaplier* feature to increase non-jackpot prizes by two, three, four or five times; it costs an additional $1 per play. Before each Mega Millions drawing, the *Megaplier* ball is drawn from a pool of 15 balls; five are marked with 2X, six with 3X, three with 4X, and one with 5X. The selected *Megaplier* ball increases the non-jackpot prize by its selected

designation.

POWERBALL - This is another big jackpot lottery game that is available in 44 states, Washington D.C., the Virgin Islands, and Puerto Rico. Jackpots start at $40 million and increase each game if there are no winners. To play, you pick five numbers ranging from 1-69 and one *Powerball* number ranging from 1-26. Each game cost is $2 to play. Drawings are bi-weekly on Wednesdays and Saturdays at 10:59 EST. The payout is available in a lump sum or in an annuity over 30 years. Each annuity payment is 5% higher than in the previous year to adjust for inflation. Odds of winning the *Powerball* grand prize is one out of 292,201,338.

For an additional $1 per play, the *Power Play* feature can multiply non-jackpot prizes by two, three, four, five or 10 times their
value.

LOTTO AMERICA - Another multi state large jackpot lottery. It replaced Hot Lotto in October of 2017 and has 13 participating states.

The following are some other types of lottery and gambling:

50/50 - Some lotteries are set up as a 50/50 where the total value that is raised in tickets is split, giving 50 percent for prizes and 50 percent to the organizer. These are usually held at fundraisers for charities or at private functions.

KENO - Keno is a lottery/bingo type gambling game most often played in casinos. To play, you select 20 numbers ranging from 1-80, and then 20 numbered ping-pong type balls are chosen out of 80 from a "bubble," which is a glass enclosure used to randomly dispense the balls. It is virtually impossible to select 20 correct numbers (1 in 3.5 quintillion). The casinos also select how many matching numbers are needed to win a prize, ranging anywhere from 0-20. The payouts vary according to the amount of players and the number of winning combinations.

BINGO - To play, you purchase cards with 25 numbers randomly printed on them in a grid pattern. Numbers ranging from 1-75 are randomly pulled from a basket or bubble one at a time. As these numbers are revealed, you mark the corresponding number on your card. To win, you need five across, down or diagonal. Once you accomplish this you must then call out "Bingo." Bingo is played mainly by church and charity organizations, and some casinos. There are about 5.52×10^{26} (exactly $15^5 \times 14^5 \times 13^5 \times 12^5 \times 11^4$) possible patterns of the numbers on a bingo card.

Millions of people across the nation play lotteries on a daily basis. Contrary to popular belief that they are played to win a specific prize, they are usually played to experience the thrill and fantasize about the possibility of becoming extremely wealthy. Hence the lottery is played as a fee to play a fun game, even though the chances of winning are slim.

Though this book references NYS lottery **games specifically, many** other state lotteries **may** have the same or similar games and also offer different games. The rules to play and odds of winning are also different depending on the state that the game is being played in.

With today's super fast, highly efficient computers and internet technology, the lottery tickets are sold and scanned in large volume. These computers also allow players to select a *Quick Pick* method for picking numbers. If this option is selected, the computer then randomly picks the necessary numbers for your wager.

Speculation vs. Investment

Playing the lottery is not an investment; the lottery is purely speculative. Though the financial outlay to play is low, the risks (loss of funds) are extremely high.

An investment is based on sound fundamentals and analysis. Investments cost are higher but offer a lower risk of loss.

"A fool and his money are soon parted."
-Thomas Tusser

"There's a sucker born every minute..."
-David Hannum

2

History of the Lottery

"The greatest advantage in gambling lies in not playing at all."
-Girolamo Cardano

"The better the gambler, the worse the man."
-Publius Syrus

It is reported that the earliest traces of the lottery date back to the Han Dynasty circa 200 BC, where they discovered ancient keno slips. These early lotteries were used to finance government projects, such as the Great Wall of China. There are also many other earlier recordings of the lottery, including its usage in the ancient Roman Empire. During Roman times they found "knuckle bones" of sheep, believed to be used as dice to gamble with.

Publius Cornelius Tacitus (54 - 117 AD), was a Roman senator and historian. In his book titled *Germany*, about the Germans and gambling, he writes:

"What is marvellous, playing at dice is one of their most serious employments; and even sober, they are gamesters: nay, so desperately do they venture upon the chance of winning or losing, that when their whole substance is played away, they stake their liberty and their persons upon one and the last throw. The loser goes calmly into voluntary bondage. However younger he be, however stronger, he tamely suffers himself to be bound and sold by the winner."

In 1434, the Dutch were recorded as the earliest public lottery system, which was held in the town of Sluis.

After this, other European towns in Flanders were recorded to offer lottery tickets for sale with prizes in the form of money.

The Dutch were the first to shift the lottery to monetary prizes alone. These prizes were based on odds and approximately one in four tickets was a prize winner. The lottery became very popular, and was considered a painless form of taxation. In the Netherlands, the lottery was used to raise money for helping poor people and to support local projects such as dikes. The Dutch state owned Staatsloterij, is considered to be the oldest existing lottery system.

Girolamo Cardano (1501-1576) studied probabilities in the 16th century and wrote a book (published posthumously) titled *Liber de Ludo Aleae* or *Book on Games of Chance*. In his book, he expressed a rough concept of mathematical expectations, derived power of laws for repetitive events, and conceived the definition of probability as a frequency ratio. With his knowledge of probability, Cardano went on to predict the death of frail-15-year old Edward VI of England. Cardano predicted Edward VI to live to his 55th year, 3rd month, and 17th day. Edward VI proved him wrong and died the next year at age 16. Cardano then predicted the date of his own death. When this date arrived, Cardano found he was still healthy, and not to be wrong twice, took matters in his own hands and committed suicide. At least with gambling and/or playing the lottery, your death is not a choice, unless you're playing *Russian Roulette*.

In the year 1566, the first officially recorded lottery in England was chartered by Queen Elizabeth I, and was drawn in 1569. This lottery was developed to raise money for the "reparation of the havens and strength of the Realme, and towardes such other publique good workes." Every ticket holder won a prize, and the total value of the prizes equaled the money collected. Prizes were in many different forms such as silver plates and/or other valuable items. Many private lotteries were held, including raising money for the Virginia Company of London to support its settlement in America at Jamestown. The lottery in England ran for over 250 years until 1826 when it was abolished by parliament.

Lotteries even appeared in colonial America and played a significant role in the financing of both private and public ventures. Between the years of 1744 - 1776 more than 200 lotteries were used to help finance major projects that included roads, libraries, churches, colleges, canals, and bridges. Princeton and Columbia Universities, and the University of Pennsylvania were financed by lotteries.

In 1768 George Washington ran the Mountain Road Lottery which turned out to be a failure. If you now own one of these rare lottery tickets bearing George Washington's signature, they are worth about $15,000. Washington was also a manager for Col. Bernard Moore's "Slave Lottery" in 1769. The prizes were advertised in the Virginia Gazette, and consisted of land and slaves.

The Continental Congress used lotteries to raise money to support the Colonial Army at the beginning of the Revolutionary War. Alexander Hamilton wrote that lotteries should be kept simple, and that "Everybody...would prefer a small chance of winning a great deal to a great chance of winning little." Taxes were generally not accepted as a way to raise money for public projects. This lead to the widespread belief that lotteries are a hidden form of taxation.

As the Revolutionary War ended, various states used lotteries to fund numerous public projects. For many years these lotteries were highly successful and contributed to the nation's rapid growth.

Lotteries eventually became a cause of financial mismanagement and corruption and, as a result, a majority of state constitutions banned lotteries toward the end of the nineteenth century. U.S. President Benjamin Harrison sent a message to Congress on July 29, 1890, demanding "severe and effective legislation" against lotteries. Congress acted promptly, and banned the U.S. mail from delivering lottery tickets. By the year 1900 all lotteries were terminated in the United States after the Supreme Court upheld the law in 1892.

Lotteries were brought back again in 1964, starting with New Hampshire. It then took many years of constitutional amendments by various other states before the lotteries reached the level of prosperity that they are at today.

"Luck never gives; it only lends."
-Swedish proverb

"The lottery is a tax on people who flunked math."
-Monique Lloyd

3

Morality

"Dear Lord, help me break even. I need the money."
-Author unknown

Religions worldwide have varying opinions on gambling, with most generally seeing gambling as immoral and sinful.

Buddhism:

Buddhism generally places gambling into three classes:
Recreational, habitual, and addictive.
Whereas recreational and habitual gambling are not a major issue, Buddha specifically spoke about addictive gambling:

"There are these six dangers of being addicted to gambling. In winning one begets hatred; in losing one mourns the loss of one's wealth; one's word is not accepted in court; one is avoided by both friends and officials; one is not sought after for marriage because people say a gambler cannot support a wife." (D.III,183)

Christianity:

Jesus taught his followers that loving God and others was more important than chasing money. This means that he likely wouldn't have approved of gambling with the sole intent to win money.

The New Testament fails to specifically address gambling, but it does contain excerpts that mention money and admonish greed and pursuing material wealth:

"For the love of money is a root of all kinds of evil. Some people, eager for money, have wandered from the faith and pierced themselves with many griefs."

-First Timothy 6:10

"Keep your lives free from the love of money and be content with what you have, because God has said, 'Never will I leave you; never will I forsake you."

- Hebrews 13:5

"No one can serve two masters. Either he will hate the one and love the other, or he will be devoted to the one and despise the other. You cannot serve both God and Money."

- Matthew 6:24

"You are bought with a price"

- 1 Corinthians 6:20

Hinduism:

Hindu religion specifically condemns gambling:

"Let him carefully shun the ten vices, springing from love of pleasure, and the eight, proceeding from wrath, which (all) end in misery."

-The Manusmriti 7.45

"Hunting, gambling, sleeping by day, censoriousness, (excess with) women, drunkenness, (an inordinate love for) dancing, singing, and music, and useless travel are the tenfold set (of vices) springing from love of pleasure."

-The Manusmriti 7.47

"Gambling and betting let the king exclude from his realm; those two vices cause the destruction of the kingdoms of princes."

-The Manusmriti 9.221

"Gambling and betting amount to open theft; the king shall always exert himself in suppressing both (of them)."

-The Manusmriti 9.222

"Let the king corporally punish all those (persons) who either gamble and bet or afford (an opportunity for it), likewise Sudras who assume the distinctive marks of twice-born(men)."
-The Manusmriti 9.224

> "On every man who addicts himself to that (vice) either secretly or openly, the king may inflict punishment according to his discretion"
> -The Manusmriti 9.228

> "Next, sins that make people sordid: gambling; sorcery; living by gleaning on the part of a man who has not established the sacred fires; begging alms food by a man who has returned home from his teacher's, as well as his residing at his teacher's house for more than four months..." -Baudhayana Dharmasutras 2.2.24

Islam:

The Prophet Muhammad and his followers opposed all forms of gambling. In scripture:

> "They ask you about wine and gambling. Say: 'In them both lies grave sin, though some benefit, to mankind. But their sin is more grave than their benefit."
>
> - Qur'an, 2:219 (al-Baqara)

> "O believers, wine and gambling, idols and divining arrows are an abhorrence, the work of Satan. So keep away from it, that you may prevail. Satan only desires to arouse discord and hatred among you with wine and gambling, and to deter you from the mention of God and from prayer. Will you desist?"
>
> - Qur'an, Sura 5:90-91 (Al-Ma'ida)

> *Narrated Abu Huraira: The Prophet said, "Whoever swears saying in his oath. 'By Al-lat and al-Uzza,' should say, 'None has the right to be worshipped but God; and whoever says to his friend, 'Come, let me gamble with you,' should give something in charity."*
>
> *- Sahih Bukhari, Book 78 (Oaths and Vows), hadith 645*

There are two exceptions where the Prophet Muhammad allowed gambling.

> *"Wagers are allowed only for racing camels or horses, or shooting arrows"*
>
> *- Sunan Abi Dawud*

Judaism:

The Old Testament of the Bible does not mention gambling but has one scripture that references to money:

> *"He who loves money will not be satisfied with money, nor he who loves abundance with its income. This too is vanity."*
>
> *- Ecclesiastes 5:10*

There are some various opinions from history and Rabbis on gambling. The Talmud thought of gambling as a sin and found it akin to stealing and thievery.

Historically, older Jewish civilizations used excommunication, flagellation, fines, and the denial of synagogue honors as common penalties for those who transgressed gambling regulations. Compulsive gamblers were described as sinners, charged with harming family life and forgetting God. Their habit has been described as abominable, ugly, frivolous, and morally impure.

The following commentary on the Torah by the medieval authority Rabbi Jacob ben Asher; Moses warned the Jewish people before his death not to become corrupted by gambling.

Politics:

Politically, lotteries and gambling have been a great resource for generating tax revenue for governments.

Is the Lottery Capitalistic or Socialistic?

Winston Churchill's definition fits both perfectly: "The inherent vice of capitalism [or lottery] is the unequal sharing of blessings. The inherent virtue of Socialism [or lottery] is the equal sharing of miseries."

In a way it is funny how we complain about big business being evil and destroying America, but we don't consider the damage from the lottery. At least when you spend money at a big business store for a purchase you receive something in return. In the lottery, the money is spent on h*ope* or a d*ream* with a negative return.

Gambling Addiction:

Problem gamblers have a significant effect on society as they have higher rates of:

- Debt and bankruptcies
- Divorce and other family issues
- Substance abuse, especially alcohol and tobacco
- Mental health issues, especially depression and suicide
- Poor physical health
- Crime

Studies have shown that two out of three gambling addicts have engaged in illegal activities to pay off their debts.

Impulsive gamblers also rate high on other impulsive activities, such as impulsive stealing, shopping, eating, and sexual behavior.

Pascal's Wager is a suggestion posed by the French philosopher Blaise Pascal that states that even though the existence of God cannot be determined through reason, a person should wager as though God exists, because if he does exist you win, and if not, you have nothing to lose; therefore if you must gamble, always take the safe bet.

So with that in mind, gambling of any kind should be avoided.

"You cannot beat a roulette table unless you steal money from it."
-Albert Einstein

4

Mentality

"Insanity: doing the same thing over and over again and expecting different results."
-Author unknown

Gambling is the wagering of money or something of value (referred to as "the stakes") on an event with an uncertain outcome, with the primary intent of winning money or material goods. Gambling thus requires three elements be present: consideration, risk (chance), and a prize: playing games of chance for money or taking risky action in the hope of a desired result. Gambling exists in all societies, and most people have gambled at some point in their lives.

A prominent California psychoanalyst, Dr. Ralph Greenson, has divided gamblers into three groups: the normal person, or diversion gambler, who gambles for diversion and usually can stop when he wishes; the professional gambler, who selects gambling as his means of earning a livelihood; and the neurotic gambler, who gambles because he is driven by unconscious needs and is unable to stop. A neurotic gambler either feels lucky or wants to test his luck. Winning gives him a sense of power. He feels pleased, like a baby feeding at a breast. A neurotic gambler always loses because he tries to re-create that omnipotent feeling of bliss instead of concentrating on a realistic long-term game plan.

Dr. Sheila Blume, director of the compulsive gambling program at South Oaks Hospital in New York, calls gambling "an addiction without a drug." Most men gamble for the action. Women gamble as a means of escape. Gambling losers usually hide their losses and try to look and act like winners, and are often plagued by self-doubt.

Austrian neurologist and the founder of psychoanalysis Sigmund Freud, has theorized a a direct relationship with compulsive gambling and masturbation. This is written about in his essay *Dostoevsky and Parricide*. Freud also wrote in a letter to his friend, Wilhelm Fleiss, that gambling and other addictions are substitutes for masturbation.

> *"Humans are pattern seeking animals. Psychologists have shown that if you present people with a random sequence, and tell them that it's unpredictable, they will nevertheless insist on trying to guess what is coming next. What the next roll of the dice will be. When the next hit by a baseball player will be. Or what next winning numbers in the lottery will be, etc.,"*
> *- The Intelligent Investor, Benjamin Graham*

Electronic Crack:
Of all types of gambling, slot machines are the most addictive. The machine is designed or programmed to maximize the amount of time you spend playing. A 2001 study by psychiatrist Dr. Hans Breiter at Massachusetts General Hospital in Boston confirmed the term "electronic crack" for playing the slot machine. Using MRI scanners on people playing slots, the brain's neural circuits fired in a way that is very similar to someone using cocaine.

The lottery is also considered a prayer against poverty, as most players are poor. This is what researchers call the *desperation hypothesis*: whereas lottery ticket sales rise with increases in the poverty rate, the state lotteries are then making their most hopeless citizens addicted to gambling to pay for government services.

Simple Thought Experiment, the author asks which would happen first: you would win the lottery jackpot or you would die from a complication of smoking over 50 years.

Starting at age 20, every day you went to the convenience store and purchased $10 worth of lottery tickets and $10 worth of cigarettes. You continued the use of the cigarettes and played the lottery for 50 years.

He concluded that, statistically, you're 50 times more likely to die from a smoking-related issue than to win the lottery.

(From website http://figuretheodds.org/)

Another internet article where a teacher played a wager type game with his high school students:

The game is a simple auction and the winner would win $50. Bidding started at $1 and all bids had to be in increments of $1. The catch is that everyone pays their bid amount whether they win or not. The teacher stopped the game when the highest bid was at $75. The students were willing to go higher because nobody wants to lose any money and have nothing to show for it. The game showed that if they kept bidding they were only throwing more money at a very bad decision. At the end, the high bidder wanted to get paid, but was reminded of the rules that every prior bid had to be paid to have a payout.

If money was collected at every bid and then stopped at $75 the amount collected would total $2,860.

Bid	$ Bid	Total	
1	$1	$1	
2	$2	$3	(1st & 2nd bids added)
3	$3	$6	(all 3 bids combined)
4	$4	$10	(all 4 bids combined)
5	$5	$115	(all 5 bids combined)
10	$10	$55	(all 10 bids combined)
20	$20	$220	(all 20 bids combined)
50	$50	$1285	(all 50 bids combined)
75	$75	$2860	(all 75 bids combined)

(From http://taylormadeforhim.com)

"Perhaps we vote in the same spirit in which we buy lottery tickets. After all, your chances of winning a lottery and affecting an election are pretty similar."
-Author unknown

5

Who Plays the Lottery

"Money is good for nothing unless you know the value of it by experience. Give a boy $20,000 and put him in business, and the chances are that he will lose every dollar of it before he is a year older. Like buying a ticket in the lottery, and drawing a price, it is easy come, easy go. He does not know the value of it; nothing is worth anything, unless it costs effort."
-P.T. Barnum

A recent Gallup Poll on "Gambling in America" found that 57 percent of American adults reported buying a lottery ticket in the past 12 months. It is also reported that the average American today spends more on the lottery than reading materials and at movie theaters combined.

The total New York census is approximately 19.9 million, so if you subtract all persons under the age of 18 (24 percent of the population) and subtract all incarcerated and incapacitated persons (6 percent), this will leave a total of 13.5 million persons that are available to play the lottery. If we take this one step further and subtract the persons that don't play the lottery at all (20 percent), this leaves us about 50 percent of the population, or 9.9 million people that currently do play the lottery. When you take the total New York lottery sales of $9.97 billion and divide that by the playing population of 9.9 million, this amounts to roughly $1,007 dollars per year, or roughly $19 per week, per person.

NOTE: these numbers are for lottery sales and don't include other types of gambling such as bingo, horse racing, football cards, raffles, chances, etc.

The Pareto Principle, also known as the *80/20 Rule*, which applies to the use of any product or service, is the idea that 80 percent of the sales come from 20 percent of the customers. In the lottery, this was also found to be true as shown in studies in Minnesota (20 percent of the players accounted for 71 percent of lottery sales); Arizona (24 percent of the players accounted for 70 percent of lottery sales); and in Pennsylvania (29 percent of the players accounted for 79 percent of lottery sales).

A Duke University study in the 1980's showed the poorest third of all households in the U.S. buy half of all lottery tickets.

The lottery has also been considered a tax disguised as a game with no lobby to oppose it. Companies respond with lobbyists to keep corporate taxes down. The wealthy families fund the elections to keep personal and estate taxes down. The poor, who do not typically vote nor support politicians, use the lotteries to attempt to gain wealth. Surprisingly, 25 percent of the states tax revenues are higher from the lottery sales than from state corporate income taxes.

Lottery opponents also have pointed out that unlike spending on a movie ticket, the lottery ticket is purchased from the government and is therefore a regressive tax. But the lottery is not a tax. Webster defines a tax as "a compulsory payment...for the support of government." It is not mandatory to play the lottery. The purchase of a lottery ticket is completely voluntary, and a lot more fun than filling out tax return forms.

Playing the lottery, tobacco smoking, poverty, and education level trend in a very similar pattern. Nationally, someone with a higher wealth status would have a higher education, and would be less likely to play the lottery or smoke.

Simply put, quitting smoking and gambling will put more money in your pocket, and is a very smart decision.

"Here's something to think about: how come you never see a headline like, Psychic wins lottery?"
-Jay Leno

6

Does the Lottery Bring Pleasure?

"All are inclined to believe what they covet, from a lottery ticket up to a passport to Paradise."
-Lord Byron

"The urge to gamble is so universal and its practice so pleasurable that I assume it must be evil."
-Heywood Broun

Winning the lottery is not as pleasurable as it seems, for in the book *Lottery Winners: How They Won and How Winning Changed Their Lives* by H. Roy Kaplan, the author interviewed more than 100 lottery winners in the early to mid 1970's. The jackpots varied at $50k, $100k, $250k, and $1 million, which for that time was a large sum of money. The book explains how a majority of the winners felt they would be better off without the lottery money, as their life was more enjoyable prior to winning. Their lives after winning drastically changed, but most often for the worse. They battled constant harassment at home and in their neighborhood. Their phones rang constantly and strangers knocked on their doors. They didn't even feel safe at home, requiring almost all the winners to relocate to a new location. They also lost very valuable relationships with friends and family, who thought they were entitled to some of the winnings. Furthermore, those who enjoyed their occupation and wanted to continue to work were forced out in a short time.

There are numerous other studies conducted on lottery winners. Although there are small percentages that are generally happier, the vast majority feel that the lottery has ruined their once pleasurable life.

Other winners got themselves in such a financial mess that they had to sell their future earnings prematurely to companies that would buy them out of their annuity at a steep discount. It is also reported that 70 percent of lottery jackpot winners go bankrupt within a few years of winning.

Another interesting book to read on this subject is titled *Money for Nothing: One Man's Journey Through the Dark Side of Lottery Millions*, written by Edward Ugel. In his book he explains what happens to lottery millionaires after they win and how desperate they get after getting into financial problems.

Happiness isn't about money. Studies have shown that the things that bring true happiness are family, close friends, faith, religion, spirituality, and helping others.

In the book *The Pursuit of Happiness-Who is Happy and Why*, David G Myers, Ph.D. concludes that doing the following things are what make people happy:

- ❖ Staying fit and healthy
- ❖ Setting realistic goals and expectations
- ❖ Having a positive self-esteem
- ❖ Having a feeling of control
- ❖ Being optimistic and outgoing
- ❖ Having supportive friends that enable companionship and confiding
- ❖ A socially intimate/sexually warm equitable marriage
- ❖ Doing challenging work
- ❖ Participating in active leisure followed by adequate rest and retreat
- ❖ Following a faith that entails communal support, purpose, acceptance, outward focus, and hope.

Money, therefore, only gives happiness temporarily, and shouldn't be desired for your lifetime goals.

"In this world there are only two tragedies. One is not getting what one wants, and the other is getting it."
-Oscar Wilde

7

Consequences of the Lottery (Gambling)

"Gambling: the sure way of getting nothing for something."
-Wilson Mizner

"In a bet there is a fool and a thief."
-Proverb

Gambling is a serious problem nationwide, for it is very addictive and controlling. Once someone gets caught up in gambling, he often will place important things to the side and his life will start to fall apart. If the gambler doesn't quit, or receive help to stop, he'll get into gambling too deep and will borrow money or take out loans to cover his losses. This eventually leads to large sums of debt and even depression. But the gambler becomes so addicted,' he can't help himself and he will wager more, always thinking that this is the time he will hit it big and thus solve all his problems. Eventually something has to give, and the end results are not usually pleasant. The typical consequences may be depression, bankruptcy, divorce, loss of their home, wage garnishment, loss of their job, or a combination of several of these. Gamblers more commonly tend to turn to alcohol and/or drugs to help them cope as their life falls apart.

Studies have shown that suicide attempts for gamblers are higher than that of any other addictions. The average rate of divorce for problem gamblers is nearly double that of a non-gambler and 65 percent of pathological gamblers commit crimes to support their gambling habit.

In recent investigations, some lottery ticket winners were scammed out of their winning tickets after having a store clerk scan to check if the ticket was a winner.

In 2006, Bob Sehested of Van Nuys, California, asked a store clerk to check his ticket. The clerk told him he won $4 and paid him. After an investigation to a false lottery claim, lottery officials paid Sehested the original winning amount of $530,858.

In 2009, Willis Willis of Grand Prairie, Texas also asked the clerk to check his tickets for winners. The clerk Pankaj Joshi, told him he only had a $2 winning ticket. The winning ticket was actually for $1 million dollars. Texas Lottery provided evidence leading to the indictment of Joshi. Oddly, lottery officials said the money belonged to the clerk, Joshi. The Texas lottery was eventually overruled when a judge issued a court order awarding Willis about $400,000 that had been frozen in Joshi's bank accounts. Pankaj Joshi, who is still a fugitive, has taken the remaining $350,000 out the country. Unfortunately for Willis, the Texas lottery won't make up the difference, and if Joshi is apprehended there most likely will be no money to recover.

Dateline Investigation:

A 2009 Dateline investigation, *How Lucky Can You Get? The Hansen Files* uncovered some unscrupulous lottery clerks in the states of California and New York.

In an undercover sting operation, California Lottery investigators would pose as customers and attempt to redeem winning tickets. The undercover investigator wears a hidden camera to record video and audio for evidence. He asks the store clerk to check his tickets, which includes one winning scratch-off ticket. The winning scratch-off ticket is made specially for this investigation. When a clerk scans a ticket, it shows up as a winner or loser immediately. The clerk even gets a printed hard copy so there's no doubt.

In California more than 600 stores were checked, and found that clerks mishandled the winning ticket more than 70 times, an 11.5 percent failure rate. All offenders in California were prosecuted and stores lost their licenses to sell lottery tickets.

Interestingly, in New York, state lottery officials got offended by Dateline and wouldn't participate. New York Lottery then sent out an alert to every lottery vendor in the New York City area. It said, "WARNING: NBC NEWS IS TRYING TO TRICK LOTTERY RETAILERS INTO STEALING WINNING TICKETS."

New York has the biggest lottery in the country, and Dateline went out to 45 locations with their own hidden cameras.

New York had at least 22 locations, or 50 percent where an undercover producer went into the store with a winning $500 ticket, only to have the clerk say it wasn't a winner. Oddly, the ticket was given back as a losing ticket in approximately eight cases, as the clerk either improperly checked the numbers, or just didn't want to bother doing it. In New York, a winning $500 dollar Lotto ticket was used and the numbers had to be looked up for that particular winning day. This means that if you had that $500 winning ticket and you went into one of those stores, you would still lose.

Also in New York, one clerk said the winning $500 ticket had to be brought to a Lottery office to be redeemed. He offered to redeem the winning ticket for a fee. This is called *discounting* and is illegal. Because New York Lottery officials refused to participate, there were no prosecutions, and each time the winning ticket was returned to the producer.

Between outright stealing tickets and *discounting*, the following has also been reported:

In Florida, a store owner in Bonita Springs cashed 120 winning tickets worth $600,000 dollars.

In Pennsylvania, a Philadelphia retailer cashed 18 lottery tickets in three months for a total of $45,000.

In New Jersey, a retailer cashed 105 lottery tickets for more than $236,000.

In New York, a retailer has cashed 120 winning tickets for more than $500,000.

In Illinois, four employees of the same store and five of their relatives cashed a total of 556 winning tickets for more than $1,600,000.

As far as prison is concerned, consider a few of the following cases:

On October 19, 2007 on Long Island, New York, a Director of a Catholic Charities thrift shop was arrested for stealing $700,000 dollars in cash to feed her gambling addiction. She had stolen the money over a six-year period, and said she "thought it would make [her] more lucky in buying lottery tickets." She was facing a 15-year prison term if convicted.

In a separate case also in New York, a medical bookkeeper was arrested in 2006 for stealing $2.3 million from the firm she worked for. The money was stolen over a three-year period to buy lottery tickets. At times she spent up to $6,000 a day. She is currently serving a 4-12 year sentence for second degree grand larceny.

"It was like e*lectronic heroin.* You know, the more you did, the more you needed and the more it wasn't satisfied." Maureen O'Connor, said trying to beat video poker machines. O'Connor, the former Mayor of San Diego, had played over $1 billion in bets at casinos. Her losses were $13 million, and stopped when she was charged with a felony crime of money laundering. She is accused of stealing $2.1 million and bankrupting a charitable foundation set up by her late husband Robert Peterson, founder of the food chain Jack in the Box. In 2013 O'Connor agreed to pay back the foundation and has a deferred prosecution agreement. She is currently living with her sister and as of 2019 no monies have been paid back.

Marilyn Lancelot, 83, was convicted of embezzlement and sentenced to two years in prison. She became addicted to gambling and forged $350,000 in checks where she worked. She has since published a book about gambling addiction: *Gripped by Gambling*.

Abraham Shakespeare, a 40-year-old laborer from Florida won a $31 million lottery in January of 2006. Shakespeare, who was homeless at the time, took the $17 million cash prize. Over time Shakespeare had grown frustrated with constant appeals for money from both hangers-on and strangers. He told his brother, "I'd have been better off broke," and told a childhood friend, "I thought all these people were my friends, but then I realized all they want is just money." One of these was Dorice Donegan "Dee-Dee" Moore, who befriended Shakespeare in October of 2008. Shakespeare went missing in April 2009, and his body was discovered under a concrete slab behind Dorice Moore's home in January 2010. Moore is currently serving life in prison.

Other notable people affected by compulsive or addictive gambling:

Ben Affleck - 2001 - checked into a $34,000 per month rehab for gambling and alcohol addictions.

Charles Barkley – 2006 - lost $2.5 million in six hours at a black jack table, and lost a total of $10 million gambling.

William John Bennett, American conservative pundit, known as *Americas Relentless Moral Crusader* has lost over $8 million dollars gambling at casinos.

Pete Rose, former Major League Baseball player

and manager, was suspended from MLB for life for betting on his own team. Rose, if not for the suspension would be in the National Baseball Hall of Fame and Museum in Cooperstown.

John Daly, the professional golfer, has gambling losses over $50 million over 12 years.

Gladys Knight once had a $40,000 a night addiction to baccarat. It is estimated she lost over $60 million from the 1960's to 1980's. She credits Gamblers Anonymous for helping her quit.

Omar Sharif, Actor, ran up such huge gambling debts that he told his agent he would "accept any part, just to bail myself out."

Terry Watanabe, the former owner of Oriental Trading Company, lost at least $205 million to casinos, including $127 million in one year.

Harry Kakavas, real estate developer on Australia's Gold Coast, is estimated to have lost $1.5 billion in just over a year. He often made baccarat bets worth $300,000 per hand, and he once lost $164 million during a single session in May 2006.

David Milch, Hollywood producer (*NYPD Blue & Deadwood*). The former Yale professor lost an alleged $100 million through gambling. He's has also been put on a $40 allowance by his wife to prevent him from losing money gambling.

Akio Kashiwagi was a Tokyo property developer that wagered between $100,000 and $200,000 per hand while playing baccarat. In February 1990, Kashiwagi won $6 million at Donald Trump's Atlantic City Trump Plaza Casino. In May 1990 Trump made a deal in which Kashiwagi was to play until he won or lost $12 million. Kashiwagi at one point was up $9 million but stayed and continued to play to honor their deal. After six days of gambling, Kashiwagi was down $10 million. Donald Trump then called the deal off and ended play. Kashiwagi left the casino furious with two million dollars in chips. Soon after, his $6 million check either bounced or was canceled. At his death in 1992 he still owed the Trump casino an estimated $4 million. His body was found at his Japan home with 150 stab wounds from a samurai sword.

Archie Karas, famous for his gambling, in 1992 with just $50 in his pocket and a loan of $10,000 from a poker friend, he proceeded to run this amount up to $17 million. By 1995 his bankroll was up to $40 million. He continued betting high stakes on a combination of craps, baccarat, and poker and eventually reached zero by 1996.

"Take calculated risks. That is quite different from being rash."
-General George S. Patton

8

The Purpose of the Lottery

"A race track is a place where windows clean people."
-Danny Thomas

The lottery is believed to be used solely for educational purposes, and that it covers the majority of all education costs. Tag lines like New York's "Raising Billions to Educate Millions," and South Carolina's "Big Fun, Bright Future," endorse the belief that it supports state education. In fact, New York's original 1967 slogan was: "Your Chance of a Lifetime to Help Education."

Out of the 44 states with lotteries, only 23 have special lottery education funds. The other 21 states place their lottery money into the general fund.

The states that allocated the funds for education have also used the funds for school construction and roads.

The states also decrease the state education aid amount by the amount of lottery funds it receives. In other words, the excess lottery funds are not in addition to what is allocated to each school district. The state then reallocates that money to other projects. Some states have also reduced corporate taxes by the amount of lottery education funding the state received. The bottom line is that playing the lottery will indirectly reduce corporate taxes or be spent in other ways that you might not agree on.

On their website, New York State Lottery lists their Mission Statement: *"The sole mission of the NY Lottery is to earn revenue for education. Fundamentally, the Lottery is run as an entertainment business."*

Since it's beginning over fifty years ago (1967), New York Lottery has provided over $64 billion for the state's grades K-12 public education.

In fiscal year 2017-2018, New York has provided $3.37 billion dollars for aid to education or 33 percent of the total sales of $9.97 billion.

Percent of Revenue Allocated for Education from New York Lottery:

- Instant Games — 20%
- Quick Draw — 25%
- Take 5, Pick 10 — 35%
- Numbers, Win 4 — 35%
- Mega Millions — 35%
- Lotto — 45%
- Instant Win & Promo Games — 45%
- Video Lottery (after prizes) — 50%-60%

Breakdown of New York Lottery Expenses:

- Prizes   52.7%
- Aid to Education   33.9%
- Commissions   5.3%
- Commissions - Video lottery   4.1%
- Contractor Fees & Other Expenses   2.3%
- Operating Expenses   1.7%

In New York, the jackpots for Lotto are paid out in 26 annual installments or in a lump sum payout. If you select the 26 annual installments, they then are set up into an annuity. The jackpot money (lump sum amount) is invested and you are paid the interest and principle over the course of 25 years. The first payment will be right away and then you will receive 25 equal annual payments. The payments are calculated by dividing the jackpot by 26, and then withholding the appropriate taxes. In New York, the federal (24 percent) and state (6.57 percent) taxes combine to approximately 31 percent of your winnings withheld. So if you won a $3 million jackpot your annual payments would be $115,000 and after taxes would be $79,000. The lump sum payout is generally equivalent to 50 percent of the jackpot. The lump sum payout on the same jackpot would be approximately $1.5 million and $810,000 after the $690,000 in taxes are withheld. The cash option increases the total taxes to 46 percent due to the higher tax brackets (Fed 37 percent & NYS 8.82 percent). So much for being an instant millionaire!

The following is an approximate breakdown of a typical $3 million New York Lotto sales drawing:
NOTE: all figures are approximate.

* Total sales $5,000,000
* Expenses $750,000
* Education $2,225,000
* Total for prizes $2,000,000
* Lotto Jackpot (lump sum) $1,500,000
* Total for 2nd prize winners $145,000
* Total for 3rd prize winners $110,000
* Total for 4th prize winners $125,000
* Total for 5th prize winners $120,000

For fiscal year 2018, New York State paid out $4.8 billion in prizes out of $9.97 billion in total revenue of lottery sales. This includes all lottery tickets combined, and as every game has a different payout ratio the total exceeds the Lotto payout of 40 percent.

Another way to look at it is 40 cents of every dollar played in Lotto goes to prizes. The following is a breakdown of every $1 played in a NYS Lotto Game:

❖ Amount played $1.00
❖ Expenses $0.15
❖ Education $0.45
❖ Other prizes $0.10
❖ Jackpot $0.30

Less than one third of every dollar of revenue is allocated for the jackpot. They then pay out an even smaller percentage after the appropriate federal and state taxes are withheld.

Jackpot Lump Sum Payout:

- Total collected $5,000,000
- Jackpot amount $3,000,000
- Other prizes $500,000
- Lump sum (approx 50%) $1,500,000
- Taxes (46%) $690,000
- Final paid to jackpot winner $810,000

So New York state collected $5 million in total sales, then withheld at least $700,000 for federal and state taxes, thus paying out $1.3 million in total prizes.

This is the basic weekly Lotto drawing for $3 million and a cash lump sum payout. With $5 million in total sales, in the end, the state holds the bulk of the cash.

Breakdown of Mega Millions Expenses:

- Prizes   60%
- 75% of all prize money is for the jackpot
- Retailer commissions are 6%
- Returned to lottery jurisdictions   40%

Funds are divided back by sales to the individual states to decide how the money is spent, be it advertising, administrative fees, public schools, etc.

Breakdown of Powerball Expenses:

- Prizes   50%
- Retailer commissions   6%
- Returned to lottery jurisdictions   35%
- Operating expenses   9%
   *Transfer percentages vary by jurisdiction.

Nationally there are over $2 billion annually in unclaimed winning lottery tickets. In 2017 there were 167 $1 million or higher prizes unclaimed nationally. Some of the larger unclaimed jackpot examples were: Queens, New York for $31 million in August 2006; a $77 million ticket sold in Georgia in June 2011; and a $68 million winner in New York on Christmas Eve of 2002.

In fiscal year April 1- March 31, 2018 New York had $587,571,000 worth of unclaimed lottery prizes, and after a year, any remaining unclaimed funds ($84,685,000 in fiscal year 2018) were placed back into the lottery's current assets.

The states that run the lotteries collect a huge sum of money, and only allocate small amounts for prizes. In New York, federal and state taxes are withheld for prizes over $5,000 dollars.

"Depend on the rabbit's foot if you will, but remember it didn't work for the rabbit."
-R.E. Shay

"You know horses are smarter than people. You never heard of a horse going broke betting on people."
-Will Rogers

9

Lottery as Big Business

"There is a very easy way to return from a casino with a small fortune: go there with a large one."
-Jack Yelton

It appears that gambling has turned into a national pastime, with the ability to play games virtually everywhere. New casinos are opening up in many states on a regular basis, and all the major cruise lines have casinos aboard their ships for passengers to use when they are out at sea. Another popular way to gamble is on the internet with fantasy sports (baseball, football, etc.), and playing card games such as Texas hold 'em and poker.

The most popular way to gamble is with state-operated lottery games. These games are available in 44 out of 50 U.S. states plus other U.S. jurisdictions. The amount of retail locations or *Lottery Terminals* nationwide exceed 200,000. The state of California has the most with over 23,000 locations, then New York (17,000+) and Florida (13,000+).

Worldwide Top Retailers, Including Franchises:
7-11	65,000 locations
Subway	42,400 locations
MacDonald's	37,000 locations
KFC	19,000 locations
Dollar General	15,000 locations
Walmart	11,200 locations

In comparison these six large corporations combined have over 189,600 locations.

Nationally, all lottery revenues combined exceeded $80.55 billion dollars. New York state alone (fiscal year 2017-18) had a total revenue for all lottery sales of $9.97 billion dollars. That's $9,970,000,000!

If this was a publicly traded company with $80.55 billion in revenues it would rank #34 on the Fortune 500 Companies total revenues list.

Fortune 500 Companies by Total Revenues:
Comcast	$84.5 Billion	#33 of 500
IBM	$79.1 Billion	#34 on list
Dell	$78.7 Billion	#35 on list
State Farm Ins.	$78.3 Billion	#36 on list
Johnson & Johnson	$76.5 billion	#37 on list

The state lotteries also spend a huge amount of money on advertising costs. We see commercials aired on major television and radio stations (during prime time), in newspapers, on billboards, posters, websites, and in magazines.

For fiscal year 2017/18, New York Lottery spent approximately $119.640 million or 1.2 percent of all revenues for marketing. They follow marketing strategies for their product almost identical to a large corporation, which proves to be highly effective. Their usage of flashy colors, slogans, and even catchy jingles helps to generate huge revenues for the state.

Furthermore, in 2017, nationwide-combined American state lotteries spent $942,435,000 on advertising out of the $80.55 billion received in sales. Nationally, advertising expenditures accounted for 1.17 percent of total lottery revenues. With all state lotteries combined spending $942 million on advertising costs, they would be ranked 47 out of the top 100 advertisers. At this level they are outspending the following large corporations:

Home Depot ($911 million), Progressive Insurance ($911 million), Coca Cola ($899 million), Apple computers ($896 million), Lowes Co. ($893 million), Molson Coors ($885 million), State Farm Insurance ($860 million), Sanofi ($836 million), Bayer ($807 million), Sony ($790 million), Discover Credit card ($776 million), IAC ($773 million), Citigroup ($763 million), Microsoft ($755 million).

But what affect does it have on children?

It's not much different to a child being exposed to junk foods such as sweetened cereals, candy, or using a cartoon character to promote cigarettes. Also, the lottery is not regulated by the Federal Trade Commission. The states themselves set up their own rules on lottery advertising.

Basically, it's like 18 years of mass media

brainwashing until you reach a legal age to start playing. Many people then continue to play through their senior years. With the overall life expectancy at 78.6 years for a United States resident, the average gambler will be playing for a minimum of 60 years.

The total revenue for fiscal year 2017/2018 in New York for all lottery sales was $9,970,000,000. This averages out to $191.7 million per week. Nationally, annual lottery sales of $80.55 billion averages $1,548,076,923 ($1.54 billion) per week in sales.

"There is no such thing in the world as luck. There never was a man who could go out in the morning and find a purse full of gold in the street today, and another tomorrow, and so on, day after day. He may do so once in his life; but so far as mere luck is, he is liable to lose it as to find it."
-P.T. Barnum

"In most betting shops you will see three windows marked 'Bet Here,' But only one window with the legend 'Pay Out." -Jeffrey Bernard

10

The Odds of Winning

"I figure you have the same chance of winning the lottery whether you play or not."
-Fran Lebowitz

"There are two ways to be fooled: one is to believe what isn't true, the other is to refuse to believe what is true."
-Soren Kierkegaard

Across the nation millionaires are made almost every week with lottery games.

But are they really millionaires? There are numerous stories of lottery millionaires that wasted away their fortune. It happens all the time; someone wins a multi-million dollar jackpot, has no experience managing money, and in a few short years he is broke and depressed. Remember, if you take the lump sum payout, you are personally financially responsible for planning and investing for the future. The other selection is annual payments at 24-30 years and again, if you don't prepare and plan for the future you will be broke when this annuity expires.

Everybody dreams about it at least once in their lifetime. Take one dollar or two and bet on the Lotto, Mega Millions, Powerball, or some other super jackpot lottery. Once your numbers come out, then you are "set for life." But alas, it never seems to happen. So what do you do? You play more of course! The more you play the better your chance of winning. Right?

Not Quite. It's funny that most people believe that they have a chance of winning. "Hey, someone has to win." But the lottery isn't successful for how many millionaires they make!

Lottery Jackpot Odds:

- ❖ Mega Millions: 1 out of 302,575,350 (302.5 million)
- ❖ Powerball: 1 out of 292,201,338 (292.2 million)
- ❖ NYS Lotto: 1 out of 45,057,474 (45 million)

"Being bisexual doubles your chance of a date on a Saturday night."
-Woody Allen

Consider these other odds in life:
Odds of......

- Dying from a dog bite: 1 in 20,000,000
- Getting canonized: 1 in 20,000,000
- Being an astronaut: 1 in 13,200,000
- Becoming president: 1 in 10,000,000
- Spotting a UFO today: 1 in 3,000,000
- Dying from food poisoning: 1 in 3,000,000
- Drowning in a bathtub: 1 in 685,000
- Winning an Olympic medal: 1 in 662,000
- Dying from a collision of an asteroid hitting the earth in the next 100 years: 1 in 500,000
- Being in a plane crash: 1 in 500,000
- Being wrongly declared dead by a Social Security data entry mistake: 1 in 23,483
- A child killed in an automobile accident: 1 in 23,000
- Injury from fireworks: 1 in 19,556
- Dying in a car accident: 1 in 18,585
- Being murdered: 1 in 18,000
- Bowling a 300 game: 1 in 11,500
- Winning an Academy Award: 1 in 11,500
- Getting a hole in one: 1 in 5,000
- Dying on a bicycle: 1 in 4,472
- Injury from mowing the lawn: 1 in 3,623
- Fatally slipping in bath/shower: 1 in 2,232
- Writing a New York Times best seller: 1 in 220
- Dating a millionaire: 1 in 215
- Getting arthritis: 1 in 7
- Not having health insurance: 1 in 7
- Dying from heart disease: 1 in 3
- American woman getting cancer in her lifetime: 1 in 3

The two largest Jackpots have been nearly $1.6 billion each for *Powerball* and *Mega Millions*. The total amount of combinations available for each of those jackpots are approximately 300 million, so nearly 5.5 times the total available combinations was wagered. Theoretically if you are wealthy enough to spend $600 million to play every combination for a $1.6 billion jackpot then you would be a guaranteed winner, unless you had to split the jackpot with another winning ticket.

Also consider how long it would take to play every possible combination. To purchase 300 million combinations at one per second would require 3,500 days or 9.5 years nonstop this includes betting for 24 hours around clock. Not too many millionaires will be made with these extreme odds.

When you play *Lotto* in New York, 40 percent of the total sales are allocated to prizes and 30 percent of this total is reserved for the jackpot. In *Mega Millions* 60 percent, and *Powerball* 50 percent of total sales are allocated to prizes. In comparison, at Atlantic City's casinos, payout is at least 83 percent by law. Most horse race tracks payout 85 percent. Slot machines in Las Vegas are required by law to payout a minimum of 75 percent, and in New Jersey, slot machines payout is 83 percent.

The largest *Powerball* prize was won by three tickets sold on January 13, 2016 for $1.586 billion. Each tickets value was $528.8 million. The cash payout after federal taxes were withheld was $187.2 million each. No state taxes were taken out as the winners were from states that don't tax lottery winnings, (California, Florida and Tennessee).

The largest *Mega Millions* ticket was sold on October 23, 2018 to a single South Carolina winner for $1.537 billion, with a cash value of $877,784,124. South Carolina law will let the winner remain anonymous as he/she has requested.

For the *Mega Millions*, 60 percent of all lottery ticket sales are allocated for prizes and 75 percent of the prize money is for the *Mega Millions* jackpot. According to the financial information provided by *Mega Millions*, the cash payout for the $1.537 billion jackpot is $877.7 million and the second to ninth prizes added up to $125,732,648, for a total payout of $1,003,516,772. This would make a total of nearly $2 billion collected. This equates to about $6.14 was collected for all living persons in the United States, which is currently 326 million.

So even though the odds of winning are 1 out of 302.5 million possible combinations, the winning $2 ticket was selected out of 1 billion tickets sold. The total number of winners was 17,569,644 for all prizes, which leaves a remaining 982,430,356 losing tickets.

Mega Millions 10/23/2018

Prizes	Winners	Prize Value	$ Paid Out
Jackpot	1	$1.537 Billion	$877.7 Mil.
5 Matching #'s	36	$1,000,000	$36,000,000
5 #'s & Megaplier	2	$3,000,000	$6,000,000
4 #'s & Mega Ball	419	$10,000	$4,190,000
4 #'s MB & Megaplier	51	$30,000	$1,530,000
4 #'s	8756	$500	$4,378,000
4 #'s & Megaplier	987	$1500	$1,480,500
Smaller Prizes	17,559,392	$2-$600	$72,154,148
Totals	**17,569,644**	**- - - -**	***$1,003*,516,772**

This jackpot started at $40 million on July 27, 2018 and increased every week for three months and finally had a jackpot winner on the 26th game.

PLEASE NOTE: due to the jackpot growing over many consecutive weeks it is hard to obtain an accurate number of actual games played to win the jackpot prize.

There are clearly more losers then winners in this game. For a typical New York State Lotto game with a $3,000,000 payout, there are 5,000,000 total tickets sold, that means that there were 4,999,999 losers and only one grand prize winner if one is lucky enough to have the right combination.

Playing the lottery, and/or gambling for that matter, is a game that most people should avoid altogether.

Most people who gamble play for the thrill of winning… or is it the thrill of losing?

On the following page are 1,550 asterisks. If, hypothetically, each asterisk represented a specific lottery ticket, then to win you would have to pick just one asterisk off the following similar pages:

Number of Similar Pages for

- Mega Millions   195,210 pages
- Powerball   188,517 pages
- New York Lotto   29,070 pages

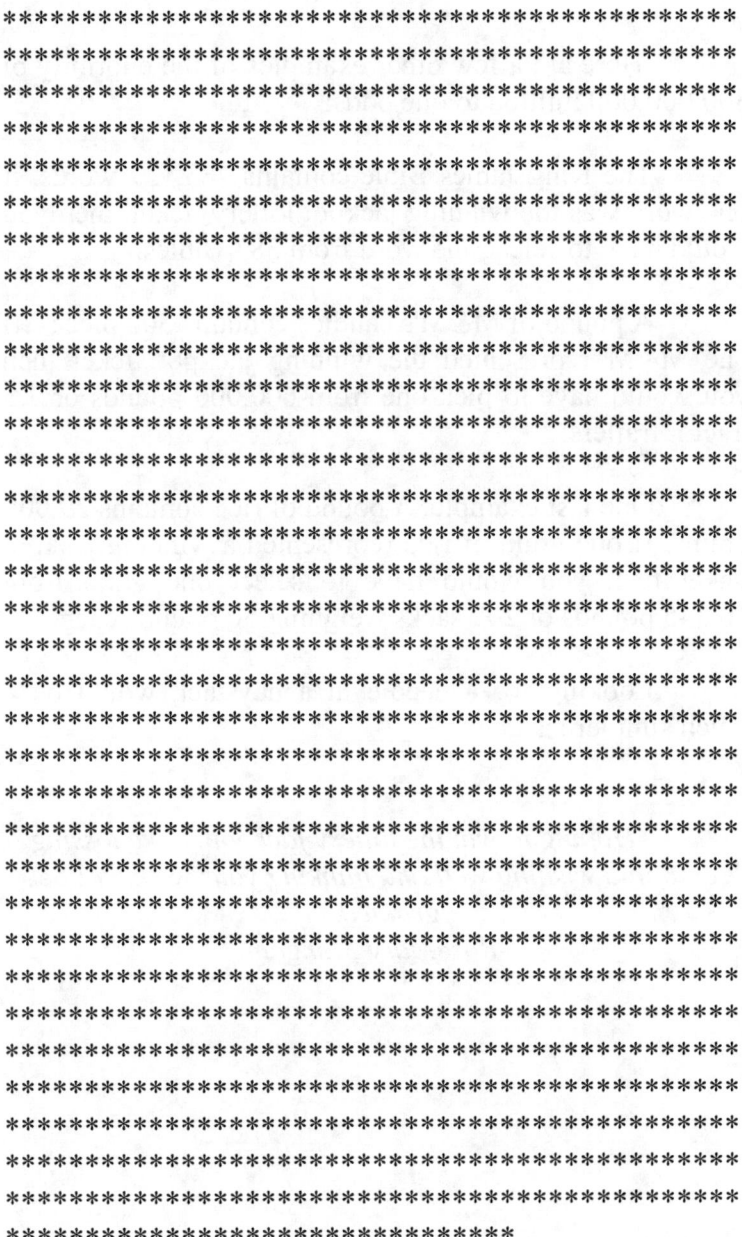

Here are a few other examples of the enormity of 300,000,000 million to one odds:

The King James Bible contains 783,137 words, if one word was the winning jackpot lottery ticket, then you would have to select one word from 383 Bibles.

A pound of M&M's candies contains 500 pieces. If one M&M represented the winning jackpot ticket then you would have to pick one from 600,000 pounds or 7.5 tractor trailers.

One last example: A pound of rice contains 29,000 grains. If one grain of rice represented a winning jackpot ticket then you would have to select one grain from 10,345 pounds or 207 sacks weighing 50 pounds each.

Looking for a needle in a haystack would be a much simpler task.

"Hoping to win the lottery jackpot is like tossing a coin in a wishing well and thinking your wish will be granted."
-RoseMary Mangam

11

The Real Cost to Play the Lottery

"He who trusts all things to chance, makes a lottery of his life."
-Proverb

"Beware of little expenses. A small leak will sink a great ship."
-Benjamin Franklin

Playing the lottery is a very expensive game that you're certain to lose at.

The first cost of the lottery is the fee to enter the game. It could be a small amount, for all it takes is one dollar (usually). But for most people that's not enough. They want to increase their chances to win and so they play more games and more frequently.

Nationally, state lottery sales per household, for fiscal year 2014, range from $100 (North Dakota) annually to $4,257 (Rhode Island). There is a wide variation on sales from state to state, and these statistics are per household. Studies have shown that two thirds of the population has placed at least a one dollar bet within any given year. Typically the lower a person's income is, the more often that person gambles.

We don't actually know the exact amount of money played by each person, but we can get a fairly accurate estimate. New York state lottery has a total revenue of $9.97 billion annually, and the state population is 19.9 million people. This averages out to $2,014 per year, per person. This comes out to a weekly cost of $38.74 that includes all minors (24 percent of population), and persons incarcerated and/or incapacitated (6 percent of population), and people that just don't play at all (20 percent of population). If we remove all non-playing persons, this amounts to a weekly cost of $19.37. If we were to add all other gambling costs, then the average person spends at least $40 weekly on all wagers. This translates to a total annual cost of $2,080! Remember this is a fairly conservative estimate, for if you apply the Pareto principle to New York Lottery, then 80 percent of the $9.97 billion in sales is played by 20 percent of the 9.9 million players. This would equal an expense of $4,028 annually, or $77.50 a week.

Across the nation $80.55 billion was spent on lottery sales (2018); if you divide this by the playing population of 163 million (half of 326 million) then the average player spends $1,977 annually on lottery.

There are also other costs associated with gambling. These include travel costs, fuel, wear and tear on your vehicle that is used to get to the store and back home, the cost of the car, maintenance, insurance, etc. To average out these costs we use the federal mileage rate for car usage which is (as of January 2019) 58 cents per mile. With the high cost of auto repairs, insurance, and fuel averaging $2.45 a gallon (January 2019) the federal mileage rate seems very conservative.

The extra mileage for players is approximately 35 miles per week, or five miles extra per day. This equates to 1,825 extra miles driven annually. At 58 cents multiplied by 1,825 extra miles, this equals $1,059 per year.

The average travel distance to work nationwide is 16 miles with an average time of 27 minutes.

Another major cost is the loss of time. Remember, time is money! This includes the extra time it takes to travel to the store, the time spent in line waiting for your tickets, the time spent checking all your losing tickets and finally the time to return home. All this extra wasted time adds up immensely.

The average time lost nationally is approximately 210 minutes a week, or 30 minutes a day, which is also a very conservative figure.

Depending on the game and the payout, the time loss may be even higher! There are large jackpot payouts where people wait in line for over an hour or drive even longer to a state that offers these games! So at 210 minutes a week, this adds up to an incredible 182 hours of lost time annually!

As mentioned, time is money. If you use that extra time to work, that adds up to 273 hours at an overtime rate of time and a half (1½). You should use this time to make money, not to lose it on a bad bet.

The national median household income is $62,175 (2018 Census Bureau) and for New York it is $64,894. With the median household income nationally at $62,175 this works out to $1,196 weekly or $29.90 per hour.

If you take the loss of time and calculate it at $29.90 per hour and at an annual time loss of 273 hours, it comes out to an annual loss of $8,163. If you make more than $62,000 the loss is even greater. Sadly, if you make less than the national average the loss is less; but living on a lower salary in today's world makes that loss even more painful.

<u>A Note About "TIME":</u>
Time is a huge factor when it comes to making sacrifices. Billionaire Warren Buffett famously said, "It's the only thing you can't buy. I mean, I can buy anything I want, basically, but I can't buy time." **Buffett is** right, we should only pursue activities with high returns and must forgo activities with low returns. An important tool that helps is called an *activity audit*. Everyone should actually take the time to figure out the opportunity costs and gains of each activity and what activity to pursue over any other. This will help avoid doing activities that have no personal or financial gain.

The "10,000 Hour Rule" is a term used in Malcolm Gladwell's book *Outliers: The Story of Success*. This rule states that world class mastery of a skill requires 10,000 hours of practice. If the annual time spent on playing the lottery was used to learn a skill, then at the end of 45 years you would nearly be a master at that skill.

Now for the real cost of playing the lottery:

If you add up all the costs, or should I say losses, you will see that the average person loses approximately $11,200 annually playing the lottery, not including any other gambling.

Some of the other costs of gambling that aren't included are sport (football) cards, football boxes, raffles, 50/50, horse racing, poker, slot machines, craps, bookie fees and any other games of chance.

This is a huge sum to play a game that you have virtually the slimmest chances of winning.

The fact is that most lottery players start playing when they reach the legal age of 18 (in most states), and then continue to play well into their elder years. Once again, being conservative, say they stop playing at age 62; this means that they were playing for a total of 45 years.

After 45 years of gambling at $11,200 per year, this equals a loss of $504,000 dollars!

So say you finally do get lucky and win a once-in-a-lifetime $3 million jackpot, then you take the cash payout option, pay your federal and state taxes and then go home with approximately $810,000 after spending an average of $504,000 betting.

The results are not so spectacular after all. The wasted time, stress, aggravation, costs, arguments with your spouse, and unrealistic dreams for a chance to win a small award aren't really worth all the trouble.

There has to be a better way.

In general, most people don't like change and aren't open to some new ideas, but the only way to *play to win* is to not play at all. That is, of course, unless you can make the odds more to your favor.

Sir William Petty (1623-1687) is considered to be the father of modern economics and its first econometrician. At one point he is said to have commented on the extent of the Irish holdings which Sir Hierome Sankey, had chosen for himself following the invasion of Ireland. Insulted, the brawny Knight challenged the near-sighted Petty to a duel, offering Petty the choice of weapons and location. When the pure blind Petty chose broad axes in a darkened cellar, Sir Hierome retreated gracefully after finding reason to reconsider the seriousness of Petty's offense.

If you feel you must wager some sort of bet, then there is one exception. There is a simple mathematical calculation you can use to determine how much you can risk based on what your net worth is.

This formula was extracted from an October 31, 2005 Fortune Magazine interview with Bill Gates and Warren Buffett. During that interview Warren and Bill were talking about their gambling wagers. Bill stated that "Warren's and my betting has always been confined to one-dollar bets." So if you combine Warren Buffett's net worth of approximately $41 billion and Bill Gates net worth of approximately $50 billion, this would equal a combined net worth of $91 billion. If typically every wager they make totals $2 ($1 bet each), then together they bet 0.0000000022 percent of their combined net worth.

The article and calculation was from 2005 and if you were to calculate this at their net worth today (2019) Buffett ($84.2 billion) and Gates ($96.4 Billion) combined net worth would be $191 billion. Their $2 wager on a combined net worth of $191 billion would equal 0.0000000011 percent.

To figure out your net worth, add up all your assets, including your home, jewelry, automobiles, cash, stocks, and any other valuables. For simplicity, take the total and round it up to the nearest million in dollars. Then take your total net worth and multiply it by .0000000011 percent and round this number to the nearest penny. For example a $1 million dollar net worth:

$1,000,000 X 0.0000000011% = 0.0011,
then round up to the nearest penny.   ---> .01

This is how much of your money you should risk in gambling.

If you would aspire to be rich like Gates and Buffett, you should value money so highly to risk as little of it in gambling at all.

"By gaming we lose both our time and treasure-two things most precious to the life of man."
-Owen Felltham

"Adventure upon all the tickets in the lottery, and you lose for certain; and the greater number of your tickets, the nearer your approach to this certainty."
-Adam Smith

12

How to Win the Lottery by Not Playing

"Two rules of investing: Rule #1 never lose money, Rule #2 always follow Rule #1."
-Warren Buffet

"Forget the lottery, bet on yourself instead."
-Brian Koslow

Here is how you can win:

Instead of spending your money on the lottery, take all the costs that are lost and invest it. If you invested the $11,200 annually in stocks, bonds, real estate, and/or certificates of deposits (CD's), and received a 10 percent return over the same time span of 45 years, starting when you turned 18 and kept it invested until the age of 62, the results would be pretty spectacular.

$8,856,980 dollars

You can see that your return would be quite enormous. Nearly $9 million is a lot better than a measly payout of $810,000.

I know this could be boring, but the payout is real. These are very minimum risks compared to gambling. A 10 percent return is a little on the high side, but not totally unattainable. A more sensible expectation would be an 8 percent return, which is what the stock market returns on average over a long term scenario.

Annualized S&P 500 Returns (Dividends Reinvested)
Over A Given 45 Year Period

Period	Return	
1974-2019	10.8%	
1970-2015	10.4%	
1960-2005	10.4%	
1950-1995	11.9%	
1940-1985	10.8%	
1930-1975	7.6%	
1920-1965	10.7%	
1910-1955	8.8%	
1900-1945	7.4%	
1900-2019	9.6%	119 years
1871-2019	9%	148 years

*Past performance is not indicative of future returns.

If you invested the $11,200 a year in an account that averages an 8 percent return, after 45 years the final total would be **$4,675,203**!

Once again, do not gamble in the stock market. Buying individual stocks and frequent trading creates risk and increases expenses. Pick a mutual fund or an exchange traded fund (ETF) that has low costs and mimics the overall market, such as the S&P 500.

As Warren Buffett and his partner Charlie Munger say, you should always invest in your *Circle of Competence*. That is, stick with investments that you know and understand. So alternatively you can invest in real estate, CDs, bonds, or treasury bills, which are more conservative, but will still provide you a nice return. The important part is to set this money aside annually, never touch it, and let it grow. If this is done every year without fail, you will prosper more than you would with the lottery.

The following is a chart depicting your possible earnings with an annual deposit of $11,200 for 45 years with a return rate of 8 percent compounded annually.

Year	Annual Deposit	Balance
1	$11,200	$ 12,097
2	$11,200	$ 25,161
3	$11,200	$ 39,270
5	$11,200	$ 70,964
10	$11,200	$ 175,232
15	$11,200	$ 328,435
20	$11,200	$ 553,541
25	$11,200	$ 884,296
30	$11,200	$ 1,370,284
35	$11,200	$ 2,084,359
40	$11,200	$ 3,133,569
45	$11,200	$4,675,203

Final Savings Balance: $4,675,203

This money could also be set up in tax advantage accounts such as a tax deferred (IRA, 401, 457), and/or Roth IRA accounts. In tax deferred accounts you don't pay taxes on this money until you withdraw the funds; with a Roth IRA, you pay taxes on the money invested in that particular year, but when you make a withdrawal all the funds (money), and all the interest earned, dividends, and appreciation are tax free.

<u>Roth IRA= $4.6 Million Tax Free!!</u>

The true winners in this game are the governments that collect a huge piece of the action on all the betting and then collect again on taxes from the winnings. But it doesn't have to be that way, you work hard for your money and it should be used for your own pleasure.

The United States is currently in a period of economic uncertainty. There are stagnant wages, inflation fears, national and personal debt are at an all time high, rising interest rates and the stock markets have been very volatile. Also, increasing health care costs and the elimination of pension plans add to this economic instability. Oddly, with the costs increasing of food, oil, gas, and other basic necessities, reports are currently showing that the lottery sales are also up nationwide. Many people are finding it hard to make ends meet and pay their bills, but then in turn they run to the store to play the lottery. If they feel that their financial situation is *that serious,* they should refrain from this risky activity and be more financially conservative. With the odds of not winning being so enormous, the lottery or any gambling should be avoided. Furthermore, by not playing the lottery, and instead investing that money, in the long term, you will become a millionaire long before the majority of all the millions of lottery players.

The choice is yours to decide...

You could play the lottery and be a guaranteed loser...

or become a guaranteed winner....

...by not playing the lottery!

Save to Win:

Another alternative is a *Save to Win* account available in 14 states at participating credit unions across the country.
From their website *savetowin.org:*

Helping credit union members save money and build wealth is a cornerstone of the credit union social mission. No matter what they're are saving for, every time a credit union member makes a $25 deposit into their Save to Win account, they're entered into a drawing to win cash prizes! Depending on the location, prizes can be up to $25,000.

Alternatively, *Save to Win* has been called:

"No-Lose Lottery"- Freakonomics
"Gamified Financial Experience"- Badcredit.org
"Safe Bet Prize-linked savings"- Nerd wallet
"A smarter way to win cash"- suffolknewsherald.com
"Lottery Savings Accounts"- gobankingrates.com
"A lottery where you can't lose"- pbs.org

"Men, who get money with too great facility, cannot usually succeed. You must get the first dollars by hard knocks and at some sacrifice in order to appreciate the value of those dollars."
-P.T. Barnum

"If you really want something in this life you have to work for it. Now quiet, they're about to announce the lottery numbers."
-Homer Simpson

"The safest way to double your money is to fold it over once and put it in your pocket."
-Kin Hubbard

Some personal notes:

This book was written with the intention to help the readers financially and to bring attention to the misconception of playing the lottery and gambling.

I have played the lottery in the past, though not on a steady basis. I have not played nor gambled since 2000. Once I stopped playing I set up an account where I deposited $365 annually, (one dollar a day) as an experiment. This is a lot less than what others are spending. Currently this account, which is now invested in stocks, has over $20,000.

Once I realized that gambling was a losing proposition, I was able to reevaluate all my personal finances.
This enabled me to reach:
1-Financial Intelligence
2-Financial Integrity
3-*Financial Independence* and thus retire early at age 50.

Being a non gambler, I was often pressured at work to join their lottery pools, especially the huge jackpots. I would often counter with a wager on my own to my coworkers: *Simple bet, 50/50 for $10, if you win the jackpot I will pay up.* For some reason they wouldn't take this bet. Needless to say, they kept ridiculing me how once everyone won the jackpot I would be the only one working, and ironically, not gambling helped me reach financial intelligence, allowing me to retire early, while my coworkers are still working.

After I retired, and being a fan of the television show *Storage Wars,* I decided to try my hand at buying some storage units. Some of the items that I found were losing lottery tickets. I thought to myself, "How sad that someone would have all their possessions in a storage unit and still resort to buy lottery tickets. If only they didn't waste the money on gambling, they might have been able to pay the storage facility and not lose all their personal property."

I personally am not totally against gambling as entertainment. As long as it is comparable to the time and dollar amount spent as in other entertainment activities. For example, watching a two hour movie at a theater for $20 is equivalent to spending $20 and two hours at a casino.

References

Web sites

bankrate.com (for financial calculators)
    http://www.bankrate.com/
New York Lottery
    www.nylottery.org/
Mega Millions
    www.megamillions.com/
Powerball
    www.powerball.com/
Gamblers Anonymous
    www.gamblersanonymous.org/
Wikipedia
    https://en.wikipedia.org/

Books

-The Art Of Money Getting
Written by P.T. Barnum – 1880
-Lottery Winners: How They Won and How Winning Changed Their Lives
Written by H. Roy Kaplan
-Money For Nothing; One Man's Journey Through the Dark Side of Lottery Millions Written by Edward Ugel
-How to Win the Lottery.... by not playing by Bill Karoshi

About The Author

Bill Karoshi is the *pen name* of the author. Bill is 53 years old and lives a private life with his family on Long Island, New York. He enjoys most outdoor activities and participating in endurance events. Bill is planning another book in the future and has retired from his daytime job at age 50.

Karoshi in Japanese translates to *"death from overwork."*

Did you ever wonder why you never won the lottery jackpot?

Are you curious where all the money that the lottery generates goes to?

This book will show you where the money goes and why you never win!

This book will also give you an alternative to acquiring a large sum of money.

www.ingramcontent.com/pod-product-compliance
Lightning Source LLC
Chambersburg PA
CBHW070439180526
45158CB00019B/1716